Awakening Grace with Jesus 2024

Embrace Each Day with Faith, Hope, and Renewed Spirit

Moses Dennis Daniel

Table of contents

Chapter One
Introduction

In the dawning year of 2024, "Awakening Grace with Jesus" beckons seekers on a profound journey of spiritual exploration and transformation. This introspective odyssey intertwines the timeless concept of grace with the enduring teachings of Jesus, creating a tapestry of enlightenment for those who seek a deeper connection with the divine.

The introduction of this spiritual expedition lays the groundwork for understanding the significance of awakening grace in the context of contemporary life. As the world evolves, so too does the quest for spiritual meaning and fulfillment. "Awakening Grace with Jesus" emerges as a guiding beacon, inviting individuals to navigate the complexities of existence with a blend of grace and the teachings attributed to Jesus Christ.

The introductory chapter sets the stage by elucidating the essence of grace—an ethereal force often defined by its unmerited favor and divine benevolence. This foundational understanding serves as the launchpad for a more profound exploration of the synergies between grace and the teachings of Jesus. In the mosaic of religious and spiritual thought, this work seeks to unveil the transformative power inherent in embracing grace within the framework of Christian teachings.

The introduction further delves into the temporal landscape of 2024, addressing the spiritual climate of the present moment. In a world marked by rapid technological advancements, societal shifts, and global challenges, the search for spiritual solace becomes both a personal and collective endeavor. "Awakening Grace with Jesus" acknowledges the unique hurdles of our era and posits that the amalgamation of grace and Jesus' teachings provides a compass for navigating the complexities of the modern world.

As readers embark on this odyssey, they are encouraged to reflect on the challenges and opportunities present in the contemporary spiritual realm. The introduction outlines the purpose of the journey—to not only explore profound spiritual truths but also to cultivate a personal relationship with grace and the teachings of Jesus that can withstand the tests of time and circumstance.

In the pages that follow, "Awakening Grace with Jesus" promises a multifaceted approach to spiritual growth. From exploring the depths of prayer and meditation to delving into sacred texts, the journey is crafted to be both introspective and participatory. It beckons readers to engage with their spirituality on a personal level while fostering a sense of community and shared experience.

What it means to be awake with grace

To be awake with grace is to embrace a state of spiritual awareness and mindfulness, guided by a sense of divine favor and benevolence. It involves a profound recognition of the interconnectedness of one's existence with a higher power, often associated with Christian teachings. Being awake with grace goes beyond mere wakefulness; it signifies a heightened consciousness that encompasses a profound understanding of oneself, others, and the world.

At its core, awakening with grace implies a deep acceptance of the unmerited favor and compassion bestowed by a higher divine force. This acceptance becomes a guiding principle in navigating life's challenges and joys. It involves surrendering to a higher wisdom, acknowledging that there is a force beyond individual control that bestows love, forgiveness, and blessings.

This awakened state is characterized by a sense of humility, gratitude, and an openness to the transcendent. It involves recognizing the beauty in both the extraordinary and the ordinary aspects of life. The person awake with grace is attuned to the sacredness inherent in daily existence, finding moments of divinity in the mundane.

Furthermore, being awake with grace entails an active engagement with one's spiritual journey. It is a continuous process of self-reflection, seeking a deeper understanding of the divine purpose, and aligning one's actions with principles of compassion, forgiveness, and love. This spiritual awakening is not stagnant but rather a dynamic, evolving experience that unfolds over time.

In the context of "Awakening Grace with Jesus 2024," this concept is enriched by the teachings attributed to Jesus Christ. Being awake with grace, in this context, involves living in accordance with the compassionate and transformative messages conveyed by Jesus. It means embodying qualities such as love for one's neighbor, forgiveness, and a commitment to justice.

Ultimately, to be awake with grace is to walk a spiritual path with a profound awareness of divine presence, allowing grace to permeate every aspect of life. It is a journey that transcends the material and taps into the eternal, fostering a deep sense of connection, purpose, and peace.

Impaction of Awakening with grace

The impact of awakening with grace is profound, influencing various facets of an individual's life and radiating positive effects on their interactions with others and the world. Here are key aspects of this impact:

1. **Inner Tranquility:**
Awakening with grace brings a deep sense of inner peace. The acknowledgment of divine favor and benevolence provides a source of comfort, fostering tranquility even amidst life's uncertainties. This inner calm becomes a stabilizing force, helping individuals navigate challenges with resilience.

2. **Compassionate Living:**
Grace inspires compassion and empathy. Those awakened with grace are more inclined to understand and connect with the struggles of others. This compassion extends to acts of kindness and a genuine concern for the well-being of fellow beings, creating a ripple effect of positive energy.

3. **Forgiveness and Healing:**
Grace is often intertwined with forgiveness. Individuals on this spiritual journey are more likely to embrace forgiveness, both for

themselves and others. This capacity for forgiveness becomes a powerful catalyst for emotional healing and the restoration of broken relationships.

4. **Harmonious Relationships:**
Relationships are profoundly impacted by the grace-centered approach. The virtues associated with grace, such as love, patience, and understanding, contribute to healthier and more harmonious connections with family, friends, and the broader community.

5. **Strengthened Resilience:**
The awareness of divine favor provides a resilient foundation in facing life's challenges. Those awakened with grace find strength in their spiritual connection, enabling them to endure adversity with a sense of purpose and hope.

6. **Empowerment for Positive Change:**
Grace empowers individuals to contribute positively to their communities and society. Fueled by a sense of divine purpose, those awakened with grace often engage in initiatives that promote justice, equality, and the well-being of others.

7. **Transformed Worldview:**
Awakening with grace leads to a transformed perspective on life. Challenges are viewed as opportunities for growth, and setbacks are seen in the context of a larger divine plan. This altered worldview promotes a positive mindset and an attitude of gratitude.

8. **Spiritual Growth and Fulfillment:**
The journey of awakening with grace is inherently tied to spiritual growth. Individuals experience a deepening connection with the divine, finding fulfillment in a purpose-driven life aligned with values rooted in grace and love.

9. **Cultivation of Virtues:**
Virtues such as humility, patience, and gratitude are nurtured through awakening with grace. These virtues become guiding principles in daily life, influencing decision-making and behavior in a way that reflects a commitment to living in accordance with divine principles.

In essence, the impaction of awakening with grace extends beyond personal transformation to create a positive influence on relationships, resilience, and societal contributions. It is a journey that radiates a transformative energy, fostering a more compassionate and harmonious existence for individuals and the world at large.

Chapter Two
The Path to Awakening

The path to awakening is a transformative journey that encompasses various dimensions of self-discovery and spiritual growth. Here are key elements of the path to awakening:

1. **Self-Exploration:**

The journey begins with a profound exploration of oneself. Individuals on this path delve into their beliefs, values, and emotions, gaining a deeper understanding of their inner world.

2. **Mindfulness Practices:**
Embracing mindfulness becomes a crucial aspect of the awakening journey. Practices such as meditation, conscious breathing, and present-moment awareness cultivate a heightened sense of consciousness and clarity.

3. **Connection with the Present Moment:**
Awakening involves a shift toward being fully present in the moment. This mindfulness extends beyond practices and permeates daily life, fostering a deep appreciation for the richness of each experience.

4. **Seeking Spiritual Wisdom:**
The path to awakening often involves a quest for spiritual knowledge. Exploring sacred texts, teachings, and engaging with spiritual mentors contribute to a broader understanding of the self and the universe.

5. **Embracing Change:**

Awakening requires a willingness to embrace change. This may involve letting go of outdated beliefs, patterns, and attachments that no longer serve one's spiritual growth.

6. **Nature Connection:**
Communing with nature becomes a source of inspiration on the path to awakening. The beauty and simplicity of the natural world often serve as a mirror, reflecting the inherent harmony of existence.

7. **Gratitude Practice:**
Cultivating gratitude becomes a transformative practice. Acknowledging and appreciating the blessings in one's life fosters a positive mindset and a deeper connection to the divine.

8. **Heart-Centered Living:**
Awakening often leads to a shift from a purely intellectual understanding to a heart-centered way of living. Compassion, love, and empathy become guiding principles in interactions with oneself and others.

9. **Inner Silence:**
Creating moments of inner silence allows individuals to connect with a deeper, intuitive

wisdom. This quietude becomes a space for insight, inspiration, and a direct connection to the spiritual essence.

10. **Service and Altruism:**
The path to awakening is not solely an individual pursuit; it extends to a commitment to service. Engaging in acts of kindness and contributing to the well-being of others becomes a natural expression of the awakened state.

11. **Integration of Spiritual Insights:**
As individuals gain spiritual insights on their journey, the challenge lies in integrating these revelations into daily life. The path to awakening involves embodying newfound wisdom and principles in practical, everyday situations.

12. **Transcendence of Ego:**
Awakening often requires transcending the limitations of the ego. Letting go of the need for validation, comparison, and self-centered desires enables a more profound connection to the divine.

The path to awakening is a dynamic and personal expedition, marked by continuous growth, self-awareness, and a deepening spiritual connection. It is a transformative journey that unfolds uniquely for each individual, leading to a more profound and authentic experience of life.

Embracing Grace

Embracing grace is a profound and transformative practice that involves acknowledging, accepting, and embodying the unmerited favor and divine benevolence in one's life. Here are key aspects of embracing grace:

1. **Recognition of Divine Favor:** Embracing grace begins with recognizing and acknowledging the presence of divine favor in one's life. It involves understanding that there is a benevolent force beyond personal control that bestows love, mercy, and blessings.

2. **Acceptance of Imperfection:** Grace allows individuals to accept their imperfections and shortcomings without judgment. Embracing grace means understanding that, despite human flaws, there is an

unconditional love and acceptance from a higher
power.

3. **Forgiveness of Self and Others:**
Grace encourages forgiveness, both for oneself
and others. It involves letting go of resentments
and understanding that mistakes and
shortcomings are part of the human experience,
and divine grace offers the opportunity for
redemption and growth.

4. **Living with Gratitude:**
Embracing grace instills a deep sense of
gratitude for the gifts of life, love, and moments
of joy. Gratitude becomes a daily practice,
fostering a positive outlook and a recognition of
the blessings that surround us.

5. **Compassion Toward Others:**
Grace inspires compassion and empathy for
others. Understanding that everyone is on their
own journey, filled with challenges and triumphs,
leads to a more compassionate and understanding
perspective.

6. **Humility in Abundance:**
Embracing grace fosters humility in times of
abundance and success. It involves recognizing

that all blessings come from a higher source, cultivating a sense of humility in the face of achievements and prosperity.

7. **Acts of Kindness and Generosity:**
Living with grace involves expressing kindness and generosity towards others. Acts of compassion and benevolence become natural extensions of the grace received, creating a positive impact on the lives of those around us.

8. **Surrender and Trust:**
Embracing grace requires surrendering to the divine plan and trusting that there is a purpose beyond individual understanding. It involves relinquishing control and placing trust in the wisdom of a higher power.

9. **Transformative Healing:**
Grace serves as a source of transformative healing. It allows individuals to heal from past wounds, find solace in difficult times, and experience a profound sense of peace that transcends worldly challenges.

10. **Spiritual Growth and Connection:**
Embracing grace is intrinsically tied to spiritual growth and a deepening connection with

the divine. It involves an ongoing journey of self-discovery and an exploration of the sacred dimensions of life.

11. **Living in the Present:**
Grace encourages individuals to live fully in the present moment, appreciating the beauty and richness of life as it unfolds. It fosters an awareness of the divine presence in every aspect of existence.

In summary, embracing grace is a transformative way of being that permeates every aspect of life. It involves a profound acceptance of divine love, a commitment to living with compassion and gratitude, and a continuous journey towards spiritual growth and connection.

Journey with Jesus

A journey with Jesus is a transformative odyssey marked by a deepening relationship with the teachings, wisdom, and love attributed to Jesus

Christ. Here are key elements of embarking on a journey with Jesus:

1. **Study of Scriptures:**
The journey begins with a sincere study of the scriptures, such as the Bible, to understand the teachings, parables, and life of Jesus. Exploring the written word becomes a guide for personal reflection and spiritual insight.

2. **Prayerful Communion:**
Prayer serves as a means of connecting with Jesus on a personal level. A journey with Jesus involves regular and earnest prayers, fostering a sense of intimacy and communication with the divine.

3. **Reflection on Parables:**
Delving into the parables of Jesus provides profound insights into spiritual truths. The journey entails reflecting on the meaning behind these stories and applying their wisdom to everyday life.

4. **Embodying Love and Compassion:**
Jesus' central message revolves around love and compassion. A journey with Jesus involves

embodying these virtues in daily interactions, extending kindness and empathy to others.

5. **Following the Example of Servanthood:** Jesus' life was characterized by servanthood. Following in his footsteps means adopting a humble and service-oriented approach to life, considering the needs of others before oneself.

6. **Learning Forgiveness:** Jesus' teachings emphasize forgiveness. The journey involves cultivating a forgiving heart, both towards oneself and others, recognizing that forgiveness is an essential aspect of spiritual growth.

7. **Seeking the Kingdom Within:** Jesus often spoke of the kingdom of God within. The journey involves seeking this inner kingdom—a state of inner peace, connection with the divine, and alignment with spiritual principles.

8. **Community and Fellowship:** A journey with Jesus is not solitary; it involves participating in a community of like-minded individuals. Fellowship provides support,

encouragement, and a shared commitment to living out the teachings of Jesus.

9. **Transformative Life Choices:**
The teachings of Jesus often call for transformative life choices. The journey may involve making decisions that align with spiritual principles, even if they diverge from societal norms or personal comfort.

10. **Reflection on Sacrifice and Redemption:**
Contemplating the sacrifice and redemption in Jesus' life offers profound lessons. The journey involves reflecting on the transformative power of sacrifice and the possibility of redemption in one's own life.

11. **Living with Faith:**
Faith is a cornerstone of the journey with Jesus. It involves trusting in divine guidance, even in times of uncertainty, and cultivating a deep-seated belief in the transformative power of love and grace.

12. **Eternal Perspective:**
A journey with Jesus extends beyond the temporal realm. It involves adopting an eternal

perspective, recognizing that life's trials and triumphs are part of a larger, divine plan.

In essence, a journey with Jesus is a dynamic and personal exploration of faith, love, and spiritual growth. It calls individuals to live out the teachings of Jesus in a way that transforms their hearts, relationships, and the world around them.

Chapter Three
Spiritual Reflections in 2024

Spiritual reflections in 2024 encompass a contemplation of the contemporary spiritual landscape, challenges, and opportunities in the context of the present year. Here are key aspects of spiritual reflections in 2024:

1. **Current Spiritual Dynamics:**
Reflecting on the prevailing spiritual currents and trends in 2024 provides insights into how individuals are seeking and experiencing spirituality in the midst of societal, technological, and cultural shifts.

2. **Technological Impact on Spirituality:**
Considering the role of technology in shaping spiritual practices and communities allows for an examination of how digital platforms, virtual gatherings, and online resources influence the way people connect with their spiritual selves.

3. **Challenges in the Spiritual Journey:**
Reflecting on the challenges individuals face in their spiritual journeys in 2024 brings awareness to issues such as spiritual apathy, the struggle for meaning in a fast-paced world, and the impact of external distractions on inner contemplation.

4. **Opportunities for Growth:**

Identifying opportunities for spiritual growth involves recognizing avenues for deepening one's connection with the divine, whether through innovative spiritual practices, community engagement, or the exploration of new contemplative approaches.

5. **Global Spiritual Consciousness:** Considering the global spiritual consciousness allows for an examination of how interconnectedness and shared values contribute to a sense of unity and collective spiritual awareness on a global scale.

6. **Interfaith Dialogue and Understanding:** Reflecting on interfaith dialogue and understanding sheds light on how different spiritual traditions are fostering collaboration, mutual respect, and shared wisdom in an increasingly diverse and interconnected world.

7. **Impact of Societal Changes:** Examining the impact of societal changes on spiritual perspectives involves reflecting on how shifts in societal norms, values, and structures influence individuals' spiritual beliefs, practices, and the search for meaning.

8. **Environmental and Ethical Considerations:**
Spiritual reflections in 2024 may include contemplation on the role of spirituality in addressing environmental concerns and ethical considerations. This involves exploring how spiritual values contribute to a sense of responsibility for the planet and ethical decision-making.

9. **Mindfulness in Everyday Life:**
Reflecting on the integration of mindfulness into everyday life allows for an exploration of how individuals are incorporating spiritual practices into their daily routines to cultivate presence, awareness, and a sense of peace.

10. **Community and Connection:**
Considering the importance of community and connection in spiritual reflections emphasizes the role of supportive spiritual communities in fostering growth, understanding, and shared experiences.

11. **Youth and Spirituality:**
Reflecting on the spiritual perspectives of the younger generation provides insights into how younger individuals are approaching and shaping

spirituality in the contemporary world, including their unique challenges and contributions.

12. **Adaptation and Innovation:**
Recognizing the need for adaptation and innovation in spiritual practices allows for the exploration of how traditional spiritual teachings are evolving to meet the needs of individuals in the 21st century.

In summary, spiritual reflections in 2024 involve a thoughtful examination of the evolving spiritual landscape, considering both the challenges and opportunities that shape the spiritual journeys of individuals in the present era.

Current Spiritual Landscape

The current spiritual landscape is a dynamic tapestry shaped by a variety of factors, including cultural shifts, technological advancements, and evolving societal norms. Here are key aspects of the current spiritual landscape:

1. **Diversity of Beliefs:**
The spiritual landscape is characterized by a rich diversity of beliefs and practices. People draw inspiration from various religious traditions, spiritual philosophies, and personal interpretations, contributing to a pluralistic tapestry of spirituality.

2. **Secular Spirituality:**
A notable trend is the rise of secular spirituality, where individuals seek meaning, purpose, and connection without necessarily aligning with traditional religious institutions. Practices such as mindfulness, meditation, and ethical living play a significant role in this secular spiritual movement.

3. **Technological Integration:**
Technology has become an integral part of the spiritual journey. Online platforms, meditation apps, virtual gatherings, and social media play roles in connecting individuals, fostering spiritual communities, and providing access to a wealth of spiritual resources.

4. **Global Connectivity:**
The spiritual landscape is increasingly interconnected on a global scale. Individuals

have the opportunity to engage in cross-cultural dialogue, learn from diverse traditions, and participate in worldwide spiritual movements, contributing to a sense of global spiritual consciousness.

5. **Environmental Consciousness:**
There is a growing recognition of the interconnectedness between spirituality and environmental consciousness. Many individuals integrate ecological awareness and ethical considerations into their spiritual practices, emphasizing stewardship of the planet.

6. **Mindfulness and Well-being:**
Mindfulness practices, rooted in various spiritual traditions, have gained prominence for promoting mental and emotional well-being. Mindful living, meditation, and yoga are embraced by individuals seeking balance and peace in their lives.

7. **Questioning Institutionalized Religion:**
Some individuals are questioning or redefining their relationship with institutionalized religion. This trend is marked by a desire for a more personal, experiential spirituality, often outside traditional religious structures.

8. **Social Justice and Spirituality:**
There is a growing intersection between spirituality and social justice. Many individuals view their spiritual practices as a catalyst for positive social change, advocating for inclusivity, equality, and justice.

9. **Youthful Spiritual Exploration:**
Younger generations are engaging in diverse spiritual explorations, often blending elements from different traditions or embracing spiritual eclecticism. They seek authenticity, relevance, and experiential approaches to spirituality.

10. **Wellness and Holistic Living:**
Spirituality is increasingly intertwined with holistic well-being, encompassing physical, mental, and emotional health. Holistic practices, including holistic healing modalities and mindful eating, are embraced as integral parts of the spiritual journey.

11. **Virtual Communities and Events:**
The digital age has given rise to virtual spiritual communities and events, allowing individuals to connect with like-minded seekers

globally. Online platforms facilitate discussions, workshops, and shared spiritual experiences.

12. **Quest for Meaning and Purpose:**
The search for meaning and purpose remains a central theme in the spiritual landscape. Individuals are exploring spiritual paths as a means of finding deeper purpose and understanding in the complexities of modern life.

In summary, the current spiritual landscape is characterized by diversity, technological integration, global connectivity, and a fusion of traditional and contemporary spiritual practices. Individuals navigate this landscape with a quest for meaning, connection, and a personalized approach to their spiritual journey.

Challenges and Opportunities

The current spiritual landscape presents both challenges and opportunities for individuals on their journeys of self-discovery and connection with the divine. Here's an exploration of these challenges and opportunities:

Challenges:

1. **Distractions in the Digital Age:**
Challenge: The prevalence of technology and constant connectivity can be a distraction, hindering individuals from cultivating deep, focused spiritual practices.

2. **Secularization and Materialism:**
Challenge: The secularization of society and a focus on material pursuits may lead to a devaluation of spiritual values, making it challenging for individuals to prioritize their spiritual well-being.

3. **Religious Intolerance and Division:**
Challenge: Despite the diversity of beliefs, there can be instances of religious intolerance and division, hindering open dialogue and understanding between different spiritual traditions.

4. **Overwhelm and Busy Lifestyles:**
Challenge: Busy and hectic lifestyles can create a sense of overwhelm, making it difficult

for individuals to dedicate time and energy to their spiritual practices.

5. **Existential Anxiety in Uncertain Times:**
Challenge: In times of uncertainty, individuals may grapple with existential anxiety, questioning the meaning and purpose of life, which can impact their spiritual well-being.

Opportunities:

1. **Technology as a Facilitator:**
Opportunity: Technology provides opportunities for virtual communities, online resources, and digital platforms that can enhance spiritual practices, fostering global connections and accessibility.

2. **Interfaith Dialogue and Understanding:**
Opportunity: The diversity of beliefs creates opportunities for interfaith dialogue, fostering mutual understanding, respect, and collaboration between different spiritual traditions.

3. **Holistic Well-being Integration:**
Opportunity: The focus on holistic well-being allows individuals to integrate spiritual practices into their overall health

routines, promoting a balanced and harmonious lifestyle.

4. **Social Justice Engagement:**
Opportunity: The intersection of spirituality and social justice provides an opportunity for individuals to actively contribute to positive societal change, aligning their spiritual values with actions.

5. **Youthful Spiritual Exploration:**
Opportunity: Younger generations' openness to diverse spiritual explorations and a quest for authenticity bring fresh perspectives and innovations to the spiritual landscape.

6. **Mindfulness in Everyday Life:**
Opportunity: The emphasis on mindfulness practices creates opportunities for individuals to incorporate spiritual awareness into daily activities, promoting a sense of presence and gratitude.

7. **Environmental Consciousness:**
Opportunity: The growing recognition of the spiritual connection to the environment opens avenues for individuals to align their spiritual practices with eco-friendly and sustainable living.

8. **Virtual Communities and Events:**
Opportunity: Virtual communities and events provide opportunities for individuals to connect, share experiences, and learn from spiritual teachers and practitioners worldwide.

9. **Personalized Spiritual Exploration:**
Opportunity: The trend towards personalized spiritual exploration allows individuals to tailor their journeys based on their unique beliefs, preferences, and experiences.

10. **Search for Meaning and Purpose:**
Opportunity: The enduring quest for meaning and purpose creates opportunities for individuals to engage in introspection, self-discovery, and a deeper understanding of their spiritual paths.

In navigating these challenges and embracing the opportunities, individuals can cultivate a more resilient and authentic spiritual journey in the context of the contemporary world.

Chapter Four
Deepening Your Connection

Deepening your connection on a spiritual journey involves intentional practices and a commitment to personal growth. Here are key ways to deepen your connection:

1. **Regular Spiritual Practices:**
Engage in daily rituals: Establish regular spiritual practices such as prayer, meditation, or contemplation. Consistency in these practices helps create a sacred routine and deepens your connection over time.

2. **Mindfulness and Presence:**

Cultivate presence: Practice mindfulness in your daily activities. Whether eating, walking, or working, bring your full attention to the present moment. This enhances your awareness and fosters a deeper connection with the divine.

3. **Reflective Journaling:**
Document your journey: Keep a reflective journal where you can express your thoughts, emotions, and spiritual insights. Writing allows you to explore your experiences and gain deeper insights into your spiritual path.

4. **Study Sacred Texts:**
Dive into wisdom: Delve into the sacred texts of your spiritual tradition or explore teachings from various traditions. Studying these texts can provide guidance, inspiration, and a deeper understanding of spiritual principles.

5. **Community Engagement:**
Connect with others: Engage in spiritual communities or groups where you can share your journey, insights, and challenges. Building connections with like-minded individuals can provide support and enrich your spiritual experience.

6. **Nature Connection:**
Commune with nature: Spend time in nature to connect with the divine through the beauty and tranquility of the natural world. Nature has a profound way of facilitating spiritual experiences and deepening your sense of interconnectedness.

7. **Gratitude Practice:**
Cultivate gratitude: Regularly express gratitude for the blessings in your life. Gratitude deepens your appreciation for the divine gifts and fosters a positive mindset.

8. **Service to Others:**
Practice selfless service: Engage in acts of kindness and service to others. Serving others with love and compassion is a powerful way to express your spirituality and deepen your connection with the divine.

9. **Silent Retreats:**
Embrace solitude: Consider participating in silent retreats where you can disconnect from external distractions and spend time in introspection. Silence creates a space for profound spiritual experiences.

10. **Spiritual Guidance:**

Seek guidance: Connect with spiritual mentors, teachers, or guides who can offer insights and support on your journey. Having a mentor can provide valuable perspectives and encouragement.

11. **Inner Listening:**
Listen to your inner voice: Develop the practice of inner listening through meditation or moments of stillness. Tuning into your inner wisdom helps you discern guidance from your higher self or the divine.

12. **Rituals and Ceremonies:**
Create meaningful rituals: Establish personal rituals or ceremonies that hold spiritual significance for you. These practices can serve as anchors, deepening your connection and adding a sense of sacredness to your life.

By integrating these practices into your life with sincerity and dedication, you can create a profound and evolving connection with the spiritual dimension of existence.

Prayer and Meditation

Prayer and meditation are powerful tools for spiritual growth, providing avenues for connection, reflection, and inner peace. Here's a closer look at each practice:

Prayer:

1. **Communication with the Divine:**
Purpose: Prayer is a form of communication with the divine. It can involve expressing gratitude, seeking guidance, asking for strength, or simply being present in the presence of a higher power.

2. **Various Forms and Traditions:**
Diversity: Prayer takes diverse forms across religious traditions. It can be scripted, spontaneous, formal, or informal. The essence lies in the sincerity and intention behind the communication.

3. **Acts of Worship:**

Devotional Practice: In many religions, prayer is a central act of worship. It establishes a connection between the individual and the divine, fostering a sense of reverence and devotion.

4. **Intention Setting:**
Clarifying Intentions: Through prayer, individuals can clarify their intentions, aligning their goals and actions with spiritual principles. It serves as a moment to set positive intentions and seek divine guidance.

5. **Gratitude and Reflection:**
Expressing Thanks: Gratitude is often a central theme in prayer. Expressing thanks for blessings and reflecting on one's life fosters a positive mindset and deepens the sense of connection.

Meditation:

1. **Inner Stillness:**
Purposeful Silence: Meditation involves cultivating inner stillness and silence. It provides a space for the mind to quiet down, facilitating a deeper connection with the self and the spiritual dimension.

2. **Mindfulness Practices:**
Present-Moment Awareness: Many meditation techniques focus on mindfulness, encouraging individuals to be fully present in the moment. This awareness can lead to a heightened sense of spirituality and connection.

3. **Self-Exploration:**
Journey Within: Meditation allows for self-exploration and introspection. By turning inward, individuals can discover their inner thoughts, emotions, and a deeper understanding of their spiritual nature.

4. **Stress Reduction:**
Calming the Mind: Meditation has proven benefits for stress reduction and relaxation. As the mind becomes more peaceful, individuals may experience a sense of tranquility that enhances their spiritual well-being.

5. **Transcendence and Unity:**
Connecting Beyond the Self: Some meditation practices aim at transcending the individual ego and experiencing a sense of unity with the universe or a higher consciousness. This can lead to profound spiritual insights.

6. **Healing and Renewal:**
Restoration of Energy: Meditation provides a space for mental and emotional healing. Regular practice can renew energy, foster emotional balance, and contribute to a sense of spiritual wholeness.

7. **Contemplative Traditions:**
Contemplative Approaches: Various contemplative traditions incorporate meditation as a means of deepening spiritual understanding. It is a path to direct experience beyond intellectual knowledge.

8. **Mind-Body Connection:**
Holistic Well-being: Meditation recognizes the interconnectedness of the mind and body. As individuals cultivate mental and emotional well-being through meditation, it positively influences their overall health.

Integrating prayer and meditation into your spiritual routine can create a harmonious and balanced approach to inner growth, fostering a deeper connection with the divine and with your own spiritual essence.

Studying Sacred Texts

Studying sacred texts is a profound and enriching practice that allows individuals to deepen their understanding of spiritual principles and glean timeless wisdom. Here are key aspects of studying sacred texts:

1. **Source of Divine Guidance:**
Spiritual Authority: Sacred texts are often regarded as authoritative sources of spiritual guidance. They provide foundational teachings, ethical principles, and narratives that shape the beliefs and practices of religious communities.

2. **Exploration of Beliefs:**
Understanding Theology: Studying sacred texts helps individuals explore the theological underpinnings of their faith. It provides insights into the nature of the divine, the purpose of existence, and the ethical framework governing human conduct.

3. **Moral and Ethical Guidance:**
Ethical Foundations: Sacred texts often contain moral and ethical teachings that serve as a guide for virtuous living. Studying these

teachings helps individuals understand the ethical principles that shape their spiritual path.

4. **Narratives and Parables:**
Learning Through Stories: Many sacred texts convey profound teachings through narratives, parables, and allegories. These stories offer metaphorical lessons that invite reflection and contemplation.

5. **Cultural and Historical Context:**
Understanding Context: Studying sacred texts in their cultural and historical context enhances comprehension. It allows individuals to appreciate the nuances of the text and grasp the cultural influences that shaped its development.

6. **Interpretation and Commentary:**
Diverse Perspectives: Sacred texts often benefit from interpretation and commentary. Exploring commentaries by scholars and spiritual leaders can provide diverse perspectives, deepening one's understanding of the text.

7. **Personal Reflection and Application:**
Applying Teachings: The study of sacred texts encourages personal reflection. Individuals can contemplate how the teachings apply to their

own lives, fostering a practical integration of spiritual principles.

8. **Interfaith Dialogue:**
Bridging Differences: Engaging with sacred texts promotes interfaith dialogue. Comparing and contrasting teachings across different traditions encourages mutual understanding and respect among diverse communities.

9. **Inspiration for Worship:**
Liturgical Use: Sacred texts often serve as a foundation for religious rituals and worship. The study of these texts can enhance the worship experience, providing a deeper connection to the spiritual essence of rituals.

10. **Spiritual Discernment:**
Developing Discernment: Studying sacred texts cultivates spiritual discernment. It enables individuals to differentiate between essential teachings and cultural or historical elements, fostering a mature and nuanced understanding.

11. **Community Learning:**
Group Study: Studying sacred texts within a community setting provides an opportunity for shared learning. Group discussions, study circles,

or classes foster a sense of communal exploration and mutual support.

12. **Integration into Daily Life:**
Practical Application: The ultimate goal of studying sacred texts is the practical application of their teachings in daily life. Individuals seek to embody the virtues and principles outlined in the texts, contributing to personal and spiritual growth.

In summary, studying sacred texts is a transformative journey that deepens one's spiritual knowledge, strengthens faith, and provides a roadmap for living a purposeful and meaningful life aligned with divine principles.

Chapter Five
Transformative Experience

A transformative experience is a profound and often life-altering event or process that brings about significant changes in an individual's beliefs, perspectives, or overall life trajectory. Here are key aspects that characterize transformative experiences:

1. **Profound Impact:**
Life-Changing Significance: Transformative experiences have a deep and profound impact on an individual, reshaping their understanding of themselves, others, or the world around them.

2. **Shift in Perspective:**
Changed Outlook: One of the defining features is a noticeable shift in perspective. Individuals often undergo a reevaluation of their beliefs, values, or priorities, leading to a more nuanced understanding of their existence.

3. **Personal Growth:**
Inner Development: Transformative experiences contribute to significant personal growth. They may prompt self-reflection, self-discovery, and the cultivation of new skills or qualities.

4. **Catalyst for Change:**
Motivator for Transformation: These experiences serve as catalysts for change, inspiring individuals to make substantial adjustments in various aspects of their lives, whether in relationships, career choices, or lifestyle.

5. **Challenges and Adversity:**
Learning from Adversity: Transformative experiences often arise from challenges or adversity. Overcoming difficulties becomes a key component of the transformative process, leading to resilience and personal development.

6. **Emotional Intensity:**
Emotional Resonance: Transformative experiences are often marked by intense emotions. Whether joy, sorrow, awe, or a mix of feelings, these emotions contribute to the profound nature of the experience.

7. **Learning and Insight:**
Gained Wisdom: Individuals often gain valuable insights and wisdom from transformative experiences. These lessons can contribute to a deeper understanding of oneself, others, and the broader context of life.

8. **Redefining Identity:**
Identity Reconstruction: A transformative experience may lead to a redefinition of one's identity. Individuals may question and reconstruct their self-concept, leading to a more authentic and aligned sense of self.

9. **Connection with Others:**
Enhanced Empathy: Transformative experiences can foster an enhanced sense of empathy. Individuals may develop a deeper understanding and connection with others, recognizing shared humanity and interconnectedness.

10. **Spiritual Awakening:**
Transcendent Awareness: Some transformative experiences have a spiritual dimension. Individuals may undergo a spiritual awakening, experiencing a heightened awareness of the divine, sacred, or transcendent aspects of existence.

11. **Narrative Reconstruction:**
Storytelling of Transformation: Individuals often construct a narrative around their transformative experience. This storytelling process helps make sense of the journey and provides a framework for understanding personal evolution.

12. **Positive Life Changes:**
Positive Outcomes: Despite potential challenges, transformative experiences often lead

to positive life changes. Individuals may emerge with a renewed sense of purpose, direction, and a commitment to living authentically.

13. **Integration and Reflection:**
Continual Reflection: Transformative experiences often require ongoing reflection and integration. Individuals may actively seek to understand, process, and apply the lessons learned from these experiences.

14. **Expanded Consciousness:**
Heightened Awareness: Transformative experiences may contribute to an expanded consciousness. Individuals may develop a broader and more profound understanding of the interconnectedness of life.

In essence, transformative experiences are dynamic and multifaceted, offering individuals the opportunity for profound personal evolution and a richer, more meaningful engagement with life.

Personal Testimonies

:

1. **Spiritual Awakening:**
Testimony: "Through a series of deep meditations and introspective practices, I experienced a profound spiritual awakening. It's as if a veil was lifted, revealing a higher level of consciousness and a connection with a divine presence that has since guided my life."

2. **Overcoming Adversity:**
Testimony: "Facing a challenging health diagnosis, I discovered a reservoir of strength within me that I never knew existed. Overcoming this adversity not only restored my health but reshaped my entire outlook on life, teaching me resilience and the importance of embracing each moment."

3. **Rediscovering Purpose:**
Testimony: "After a period of feeling lost and unfulfilled, a transformative experience led me to rediscover my true purpose. I found a profound sense of meaning and passion that has since guided my career choices and personal relationships."

4. **Recovery from Addiction:**

Testimony: "Struggling with addiction, I hit rock bottom. Through a transformative journey of recovery, I discovered a renewed sense of self and a supportive community. Each day in sobriety is a testament to the transformative power of resilience, support, and personal commitment."

5. **Cultural Immersion:**
Testimony: "Living in a foreign culture for a year opened my eyes to new perspectives and ways of life. This transformative experience not only enriched my understanding of diversity but also fostered a deep appreciation for the interconnectedness of humanity."

6. **Parenting and Growth:**
Testimony: "Becoming a parent transformed my life in ways I never anticipated. The challenges and joys of raising a child have been a source of continual growth, teaching me patience, selflessness, and the boundless capacity for love."

7. **Service and Compassion:**
Testimony: "Engaging in volunteer work in a marginalized community allowed me to witness the transformative power of compassion. This experience ignited a lifelong commitment to

service, emphasizing the profound impact we can have on each other's lives through acts of kindness."

8. **Educational Breakthrough:**
Testimony: "Struggling academically for years, a breakthrough moment during a tutoring session completely changed my approach to learning. This transformative experience not only improved my grades but instilled a newfound love for education and personal growth."

9. **Nature Connection:**
Testimony: "Spending a month in solitude in nature allowed me to reconnect with the earth in a way that transformed my entire perspective. The beauty, simplicity, and rhythm of nature became a guiding force, bringing peace and harmony into my daily life."

10. **Entrepreneurial Journey:**
Testimony: "Starting my own business was a transformative leap of faith. The challenges and successes have taught me resilience, innovation, and the importance of aligning passion with purpose. It's a journey that continually reshapes my understanding of success and fulfillment."

These personal testimonies reflect the diverse ways in which transformative experiences can profoundly impact individuals across various aspects of life.

Community Stories

Certainly, here are some community stories that highlight the shared experiences, resilience, and bonds within different communities:

1. **Unity Amidst Adversity:**
Community Story: "In the face of a natural disaster, our community rallied together to provide immediate relief and support. The shared determination to rebuild not only physical structures but also the spirit of our neighborhood showcased the strength that emerges when communities unite."

2. **Cultural Celebration:**
Community Story: "Our annual cultural festival has become a cherished tradition that brings our diverse community together. It's a vibrant celebration of our shared heritage, fostering understanding, and creating a strong

sense of unity among residents from various backgrounds."

3. **Community Garden Success:**
Community Story: "The establishment of a community garden transformed our neighborhood. What began as a small initiative for sustainable living blossomed into a space for shared learning, collaboration, and the joy of harvesting fresh produce together."

4. **Supporting Local Businesses:**
Community Story: "During challenging economic times, our community banded together to support local businesses. The commitment to shopping locally not only sustained our vibrant Main Street but also reinforced the importance of fostering a resilient and interconnected local economy."

5. **Educational Empowerment:**
Community Story: "Through a collective effort, our community secured funding for a learning center that provides educational resources for children and adults alike. This initiative has empowered individuals to pursue learning opportunities and strengthened our community's commitment to education."

6. **Interfaith Collaboration:**
Community Story: "Our interfaith community collaborates on projects that address social issues and promote understanding. This inclusive approach fosters deep connections among individuals from different religious backgrounds, highlighting the power of unity in diversity."

7. **Community Wellness Initiative:**
Community Story: "A wellness initiative brought residents together to focus on physical and mental health. Regular group activities, workshops, and support networks have created a strong foundation for a healthier, happier community."

8. **Environmental Stewardship:**
Community Story: "Our commitment to environmental sustainability led to a community-wide effort to reduce waste and adopt eco-friendly practices. The sense of shared responsibility for our planet has not only improved our local environment but also strengthened our community bonds."

9. **Artistic Expression and Creativity:**

Community Story: "Embracing the arts, our community established a mural project that transformed blank walls into vibrant expressions of our shared identity. This creative endeavor has not only beautified our surroundings but also inspired a sense of pride and belonging."

10. **Elderly Support Network:**
Community Story: "Recognizing the needs of our elderly residents, a volunteer network was established to provide companionship, assistance, and community activities. This intergenerational connection has created a sense of belonging and mutual support."

These community stories showcase the resilience, collaboration, and shared values that define the essence of various communities, demonstrating the impact of collective efforts on the well-being and cohesion of residents.

Chapter Six
Living Grace in Daily life

Certainly! Living with grace in daily life aligns with many principles found in the Bible. Here are some aspects of living grace with corresponding Bible verses:

1. **Practice Gratitude:**
Express Appreciation: "Give thanks in all circumstances; for this is the will of God in Christ Jesus for you." (1 Thessalonians 5:18)

2. **Kindness Toward Others:**
Acts of Kindness: "Be kind to one another, tenderhearted, forgiving one another, as God in Christ forgave you." (Ephesians 4:32)

3. **Mindful Presence:**

Be Present: "This is the day that the Lord has made; let us rejoice and be glad in it." (Psalm 118:24)

4. **Forgiveness:**
Letting Go: "Bear with each other and forgive one another if any of you has a grievance against someone. Forgive as the Lord forgave you." (Colossians 3:13)

5. **Compassionate Listening:**
Deep Understanding: "My dear brothers and sisters, take note of this: Everyone should be quick to listen, slow to speak, and slow to become angry." (James 1:19)

6. **Generosity:**
Share Abundantly: "Each of you should give what you have decided in your heart to give, not reluctantly or under compulsion, for God loves a cheerful giver." (2 Corinthians 9:7)

7. **Humility:**
Embrace Humility: "Do nothing out of selfish ambition or vain conceit. Rather, in humility, value others above yourselves." (Philippians 2:3)

8. **Responding, Not Reacting:**
Calm Responses: "A gentle answer turns away wrath, but a harsh word stirs up anger." (Proverbs 15:1)

9. **Cultivate Inner Peace:**
Inner Harmony: "You will keep in perfect peace those whose minds are steadfast because they trust in you." (Isaiah 26:3)

10. **Integrity:**
Live with Integrity: "The integrity of the upright guides them, but the unfaithful are destroyed by their duplicity." (Proverbs 11:3)

11. **Resilience:**
Face Challenges Gracefully: "I can do all this through him who gives me strength." (Philippians 4:13)

12. **Celebrate Others' Success:**
Support Others: "Rejoice with those who rejoice; mourn with those who mourn." (Romans 12:15)

Living with grace, as guided by these biblical principles, reflects a commitment to love,

compassion, and humility in our daily
interactions with others.

Compassion and Forgiveness

Compassion and forgiveness are intertwined
virtues that play a significant role in fostering
positive relationships and personal well-being.
Here's a brief exploration of each:

Compassion:
Compassion is the empathetic understanding of
others' suffering, coupled with a genuine desire to
alleviate that suffering. It involves kindness,
empathy, and a selfless willingness to help others
in times of need.

* Bible Verse on Compassion:
- "Be kind and compassionate to one another,
forgiving each other, just as in Christ God
forgave you." (Ephesians 4:32)

* Key Aspects of Compassion:
1. **Empathy:** Compassion involves putting
oneself in another person's shoes, understanding
their feelings, and responding with empathy.

2. **Kindness in Action:** It goes beyond feeling for others; compassion translates into kind actions and a willingness to help.
3. **Non-Judgment:** Compassion involves a non-judgmental attitude, recognizing the shared humanity in all individuals.

Forgiveness:
Forgiveness is the intentional decision to release feelings of resentment or vengeance toward someone who has harmed you. It involves letting go of negative emotions and allowing space for healing and reconciliation.

* Bible Verse on Forgiveness:
- "Bear with each other and forgive one another if any of you has a grievance against someone. Forgive as the Lord forgave you." (Colossians 3:13)

* Key Aspects of Forgiveness:
1. **Release of Resentment:** Forgiveness involves letting go of anger, bitterness, and resentment towards those who have wronged you.
2. **Healing:** It is a process that contributes to personal healing, allowing individuals to move forward and find peace.

3. **Reconciliation:** While not always possible, forgiveness opens the door to reconciliation and restored relationships.

Interconnection of Compassion and Forgiveness:
- Compassion often precedes forgiveness, as it involves understanding and empathizing with the experiences of others.
- Both virtues contribute to creating harmonious relationships, fostering understanding, and promoting emotional well-being.
- Practicing compassion can make forgiveness more attainable, as it cultivates a mindset of understanding and empathy.

Application in Daily Life:
- **Interpersonal Relationships:** Compassion and forgiveness are crucial in resolving conflicts and maintaining healthy relationships.
- **Self-Reflection:** Applying these virtues to oneself, including self-compassion and self-forgiveness, is essential for personal growth.
- **Community and Society:** Compassion and forgiveness contribute to building compassionate communities and fostering societal healing.

In summary, compassion and forgiveness are transformative virtues that not only contribute to personal well-being but also have the power to create a more compassionate and forgiving world.

Acts of Kindness

Acts of kindness are intentional, selfless gestures that bring joy, support, and positivity to others. They can be simple or elaborate, but their impact often extends far beyond the immediate moment. Here are some examples of acts of kindness:

1. **Smile and Greet:**
Action: Smile at strangers and offer a friendly greeting.
Impact: Creates a positive and welcoming atmosphere, fostering connection.

2. **Random Acts of Kindness Notes:**
Action: Leave uplifting notes in public spaces for others to find.
Impact: Spreads positivity and encouragement to those who come across the notes.

3. **Helping Hand:**
Action: Assist someone with carrying groceries, opening doors, or other small tasks.
Impact: Demonstrates thoughtfulness and consideration for others' well-being.

4. **Compliment Others:**
Action: Offer genuine compliments to people around you.
Impact: Boosts self-esteem and brightens someone's day with a positive affirmation.

5. **Donate to a Charity:**
Action: Contribute to a charitable organization or cause.
Impact: Supports those in need and contributes to positive societal change.

6. **Volunteer Your Time:**
Action: Offer your time to volunteer for a community service or charitable event.
Impact: Provides valuable assistance and fosters a sense of community.

7. **Listen Actively:**
Action: Practice active listening when someone needs to talk.

Impact: Demonstrates empathy and shows that you genuinely care about others' feelings.

8. **Send Thank-You Notes:**
Action: Express gratitude by sending handwritten thank-you notes.
Impact: Makes others feel appreciated and valued.

9. **Surprise Treats:**
Action: Surprise colleagues, friends, or family with unexpected treats or snacks.
Impact: Creates a moment of joy and appreciation.

10. **Offer Encouragement:**
Action: Encourage someone who is facing challenges or pursuing a goal.
Impact: Provides motivation and support during difficult times.

11. **Forgive and Let Go:**
Action: Practice forgiveness and let go of resentments.
Impact: Fosters personal well-being and contributes to a more positive mindset.

12. **Share Knowledge:**

Action: Share your knowledge or skills to help someone learn or improve.
Impact: Empowers others and promotes a culture of learning and growth.

13. **Plant a Tree or Flowers:**
Action: Contribute to the environment by planting trees or flowers.
Impact: Enhances the beauty of the surroundings and promotes ecological well-being.

14. **Support Local Businesses:**
Action: Choose to shop at local businesses or recommend them to others.
Impact: Supports the local economy and small business owners.

15. **Write Letters of Appreciation:**
Action: Write heartfelt letters expressing appreciation to people who have positively impacted your life.
Impact: Creates lasting memories and deepens connections.

Acts of kindness, regardless of their scale, have the power to create a ripple effect, inspiring

others to pay it forward and contributing to a
more compassionate and caring world.

Chapter Seven
Navigating Modern Challenges

Navigating modern challenges requires a
combination of adaptability, resilience, and
thoughtful strategies. Here are some insights to
help navigate and overcome contemporary
difficulties:

1. **Cultivate Adaptability:**
Approach: Embrace change as a constant and
develop adaptability. Cultivate a mindset that
sees challenges as opportunities for growth and
learning.

2. **Strengthen Resilience:**
Approach: Build resilience by developing coping mechanisms and a support system. Recognize that setbacks are a natural part of life and focus on bouncing back stronger.

3. **Prioritize Mental Health:**
Approach: Recognize the importance of mental well-being. Practice self-care, mindfulness, and seek professional support when needed to manage stress and anxiety.

4. **Continuous Learning:**
Approach: Adopt a mindset of continuous learning. Stay informed about new developments, technologies, and skills to remain relevant in a rapidly changing world.

5. **Build Strong Connections:**
Approach: Cultivate meaningful relationships. Building a strong network of support, both personally and professionally, can provide guidance and assistance during challenging times.

6. **Digital Literacy:**

Approach: Develop digital literacy skills to navigate the complexities of the modern technological landscape. Stay informed about online security, digital tools, and the evolving digital economy.

7. **Balanced Information Consumption:**
Approach: Be mindful of information consumption. Verify sources, seek diverse perspectives, and practice media literacy to navigate through the vast amount of information available.

8. **Financial Literacy:**
Approach: Enhance financial literacy to make informed decisions about budgeting, saving, and investing. Understand the dynamics of the modern financial landscape to secure personal financial stability.

9. **Environmental Responsibility:**
Approach: Embrace environmental responsibility. Adopt sustainable practices in daily life and support initiatives that contribute to environmental conservation and climate action.

10. **Professional Agility:**

Approach: Foster professional agility. Stay
open to acquiring new skills, adapting to industry
changes, and exploring diverse career paths as
the job market evolves.

11. **Civic Engagement:**
Approach: Engage in civic activities.
Participate in community initiatives, advocate for
social issues, and contribute to positive change
within your local and global communities.

12. **Embrace Diversity and Inclusion:**
Approach: Promote diversity and inclusion
in all aspects of life. Embracing diverse
perspectives fosters innovation, understanding,
and a more inclusive society.

13. **Time Management:**
Approach: Develop effective time
management skills. Prioritize tasks, set realistic
goals, and maintain a healthy work-life balance
to avoid burnout.

14. **Health and Wellness:**
Approach: Prioritize physical health through
regular exercise, a balanced diet, and sufficient
sleep. A healthy lifestyle contributes to overall
well-being and resilience.

15. **Global Awareness:**
Approach: Cultivate global awareness. Stay informed about international events, understand global interconnectedness, and contribute to efforts that address global challenges.

Navigating modern challenges is an ongoing process that involves a combination of personal development, societal engagement, and adaptability to the ever-changing landscape. By adopting a proactive and positive approach, individuals can successfully navigate and overcome the complexities of the contemporary world.

Faith in a Changing World

Maintaining faith in a changing world requires a blend of spiritual grounding, adaptability, and a resilient perspective. Here are insights to help navigate the challenges while holding onto one's faith:

1. **Spiritual Foundation:**

Approach: Strengthen your spiritual foundation. Regular prayer, meditation, and reflection provide a sense of connection and guidance, especially in times of change and uncertainty.

2. **Adaptability and Flexibility:**
Approach: Embrace adaptability. Understand that change is a constant part of life and that your faith can be a source of stability and wisdom as you navigate through different seasons.

3. **Community and Fellowship:**
Approach: Engage with a faith community. Sharing experiences and supporting one another fosters a sense of belonging and provides a collective strength in facing challenges.

4. **Seeking Deeper Understanding:**
Approach: Delve into the teachings of your faith. Seeking a deeper understanding can provide insights and wisdom to navigate the complexities of the changing world.

5. **Mindful Living:**
Approach: Practice mindful living. Being present in the moment allows you to appreciate

the beauty and blessings in your life, reinforcing your faith in the goodness of the world.

6. **Crisis of Faith:**
Approach: Acknowledge and address doubts. A changing world might bring moments of uncertainty. Instead of suppressing doubts, explore them, seek guidance, and view them as opportunities for spiritual growth.

7. **Service and Compassion:**
Approach: Engage in acts of service and compassion. Contributing positively to the lives of others aligns with many faith teachings and brings a sense of purpose and fulfillment.

8. **Scripture and Reflection:**
Approach: Regularly read sacred texts and reflect on their teachings. Drawing inspiration from scripture can provide guidance and strength during challenging times.

9. **Maintain Hope and Optimism:**
Approach: Cultivate hope and optimism. Faith is often intertwined with hope, and maintaining a positive outlook can be a testament to your trust in a higher purpose.

10. **Dialogue and Understanding:**
Approach: Engage in interfaith dialogue and seek to understand diverse perspectives. This fosters tolerance, unity, and a broader appreciation for the diversity of beliefs in our changing world.

11. **Balancing Tradition and Progress:**
Approach: Find a balance between tradition and progress. Embrace positive aspects of change while holding onto the core values and traditions that anchor your faith.

12. **Mind-Body Connection:**
Approach: Recognize the mind-body connection. Practices such as yoga or mindful breathing can enhance your spiritual well-being and help navigate the stresses of a changing world.

13. **Prayer and Guidance:**
Approach: Turn to prayer for guidance. Trusting in a higher power and seeking divine wisdom can provide solace and direction during times of uncertainty.

14. **Environmental Stewardship:**

Approach: Embrace environmental stewardship. Many faith traditions emphasize the importance of caring for the Earth, aligning with efforts to address global challenges like climate change.

15. **Gratitude Practices:**
Approach: Cultivate gratitude. Regularly expressing thanks for the blessings in your life can foster a positive mindset and deepen your connection to your faith.

In essence, maintaining faith in a changing world involves a dynamic interplay between spiritual practices, personal growth, and a compassionate engagement with the evolving global landscape.

Overcoming Doubts

Overcoming doubts is a common part of the human experience, and it involves a process of self-reflection, seeking understanding, and finding ways to reinforce your beliefs. Here are some strategies to help overcome doubts:

1. **Acknowledge and Accept Doubts:**
Approach: Recognize that doubt is a natural aspect of faith and personal growth. Accepting doubts without judgment allows for a healthier exploration of your beliefs.

2. **Seek Knowledge and Understanding:**
Approach: Engage in learning more about your faith or the subject of your doubts. Seeking knowledge and understanding can provide clarity and strengthen your convictions.

3. **Open Dialogue:**
Approach: Engage in open and honest conversations with individuals who share your faith or those who hold different beliefs. Dialogue can offer diverse perspectives and insights.

4. **Consult Spiritual Leaders:**
Approach: Seek guidance from spiritual leaders, mentors, or individuals well-versed in your faith. Their wisdom and experiences may provide valuable perspectives on navigating doubts.

5. **Reflect on Personal Experiences:**

Approach: Reflect on your personal experiences and the moments that reaffirmed your faith. Revisiting these moments can serve as anchors during times of doubt.

6. **Explore Spiritual Practices:**
Approach: Engage in spiritual practices such as prayer, meditation, or rituals. These practices can create a deeper connection with your faith and offer moments of introspection.

7. **Read Sacred Texts:**
Approach: Read and reflect on the sacred texts of your faith. Often, the teachings within these texts provide guidance and answers to common questions and doubts.

8. **Connect with a Faith Community:**
Approach: Share your doubts with a supportive faith community. Being part of a community can provide encouragement, shared experiences, and a sense of belonging.

9. **Examine Personal Values:**
Approach: Examine your personal values and how they align with your faith. Identifying the core values that resonate with you can strengthen your commitment to your beliefs.

10. **Understand Faith as a Journey:**
Approach: Consider faith as a journey rather than a destination. Embracing the evolving nature of faith allows for growth and development, acknowledging that doubts can be part of the process.

11. **Prayer for Guidance:**
Approach: Turn to prayer for guidance. Express your doubts and uncertainties in prayer, seeking divine wisdom and a sense of inner peace.

12. **Learn from Doubt:**
Approach: Consider doubts as opportunities for personal and spiritual growth. Embracing doubt can lead to a deeper, more nuanced understanding of your faith.

13. **Balance Reason and Faith:**
Approach: Seek a balance between reason and faith. Understand that faith and reason can coexist, and exploring questions with a thoughtful and open-minded approach can lead to resolution.

14. **Practice Patience:**

Approach: Be patient with yourself. Overcoming doubts is a gradual process, and allowing yourself the time and space to navigate these uncertainties is important.

15. **Find Comfort in Community:** *Approach:* Find comfort in the shared experiences of your faith community. Knowing that others have faced similar doubts and overcome them can be reassuring.

Remember that overcoming doubts is a personal journey, and it's okay to seek support and explore different avenues to find the answers or reassurance you need.

Chapter Eight
Conclusion

In the journey of faith, doubts are not roadblocks but rather signposts guiding individuals toward a deeper understanding and connection with their beliefs. The process of overcoming doubts is a nuanced exploration that involves self-reflection, seeking knowledge, and embracing the transformative nature of faith. Here, we conclude with a few key reflections:

1. **Embracing Doubt as a Catalyst for Growth:**
Conclusion: Doubts can serve as catalysts for personal and spiritual growth. Rather than viewing doubt as a threat, consider it an opportunity to deepen your understanding and strengthen your convictions.

2. **Continuous Learning and Exploration:**
Conclusion: The quest for faith is a continuous journey of learning and exploration. Engage with sacred texts, seek wisdom from spiritual leaders, and embrace the richness of your faith community to nourish your spiritual growth.

3. **Community and Support:**
Conclusion: The support of a faith community can be a source of strength during times of doubt. Sharing experiences, seeking guidance, and finding solace in community

connections can be invaluable on your faith
journey.

4. **Balancing Reason and Faith:**
Conclusion: Striking a balance between
reason and faith allows for a harmonious
coexistence. Understanding that faith can
incorporate thoughtful inquiry and reflection
fosters a more holistic and resilient belief system.

5. **Prayer and Spiritual Practices:**
Conclusion: Prayer and engaging in spiritual
practices offer moments of connection and
introspection. These practices can provide
guidance, comfort, and a sense of peace,
contributing to the overall depth of your faith.

6. **Patience and Acceptance:**
Conclusion: Patience and self-acceptance are
essential. Recognize that the journey of
overcoming doubts is unique to each individual.
Embrace the process, allowing yourself the time
and space to navigate uncertainties with grace.

7. **Faith as a Dynamic Journey:**
Conclusion: Consider faith not as a static
destination but as a dynamic journey. Embracing
the evolving nature of faith acknowledges that

doubts and questions are integral components of a maturing and resilient belief system.

In conclusion, the path of faith is marked by a willingness to explore, question, and grow. Doubts, when approached with openness and humility, can lead to a profound and enriching spiritual experience. May your journey be filled with wisdom, understanding, and a deepening connection with the beliefs that guide and inspire you.